WHICH WAY IS WHICH?

As you follow a road in a car, left and right turns and other directions are part of what drivers must learn. It's the same with operating a boat. A boat's sides and front and back directions have names that all boaters should know. The front is called the bow. The back is called the stern. The left side is called port. And the right side is starboard. These names help keep navigation rules understood by everyone from a paddler in a kayak to a large boat's captain. If you can remember these directions, you'll know the code to navigation direction.

Unscramble the words around this boat to learn what the front, back and sides of a boat are named.

OWB

ROPT

OBADRRSTA

TRSEN

The direction at the front end of the boat is called **FORWARD**.
The direction at the back of the boat is called **AFT**.

NAVIGATION RULES

GIVE-WAY VESSEL
OR
STAND-ON VESSEL?

If you're in a boat and another boat is passing (overtaking), meeting or crossing in front of you, how do you know which boat is allowed to navigate where it wants to go? Each boat operator needs to know the Navigation Rules. The rules for when two boats meet, pass or cross identifies one boat as the Give-way Vessel and the other as the Stand-on Vessel. The boat that maintains constant speed and direction is the Stand-on Vessel. A boat that stays out of the way of another boat is the Give-way Vessel.

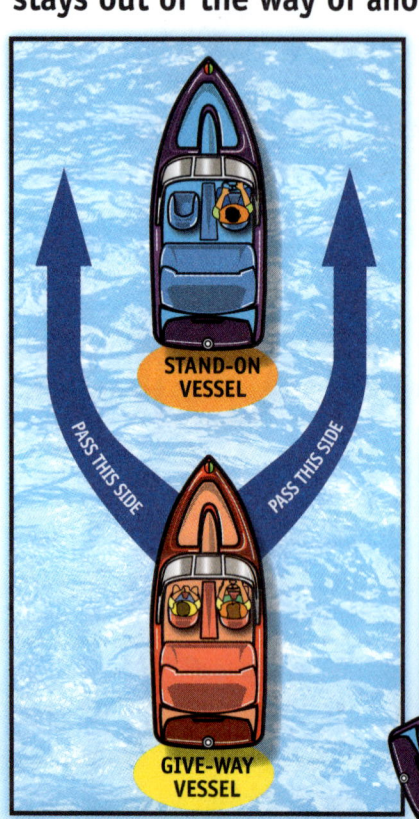

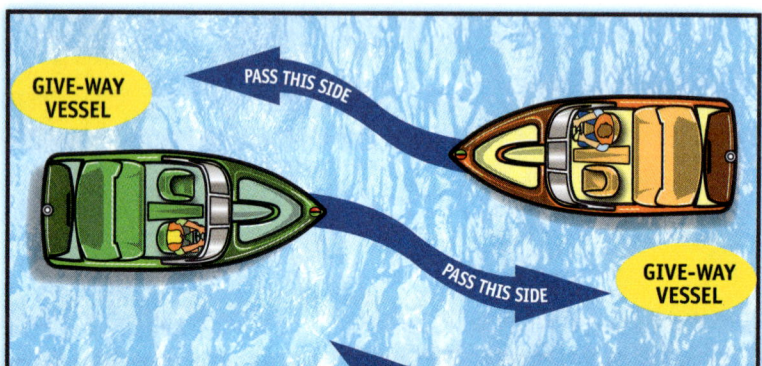

MATCH-UP
Each boat shown is like one of the other boats shown. Find the matched boats. One of them doesn't have a match.

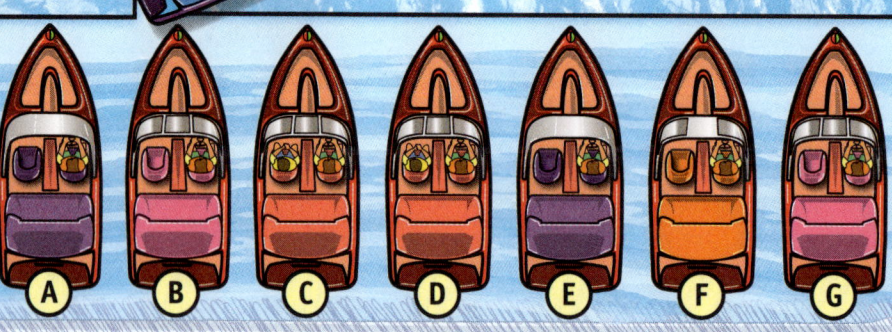

NAVIGATION RULES

OVERTAKING ANOTHER BOAT

The U.S. Coast Guard's Inland Navigation Rule #13 shows what a boater needs to do in order to properly and safely overtake another boat. Overtaking means to pass another boat. The GIVE-WAY VESSEL can pass the STAND-ON VESSEL on either side.

SOUND SIGNALS

2 SHORT BLASTS (1 second each) If a boat passes another boat on its port (left) side.

1 SHORT BLAST (1 second) If a boat passes another boat on its starboard (right) side.

Start at the top left corner and move from left to right, top to bottom to uncover the phrase. Group the letters in the same color dot, in order, to form each of the three words.

Answer on page 15.

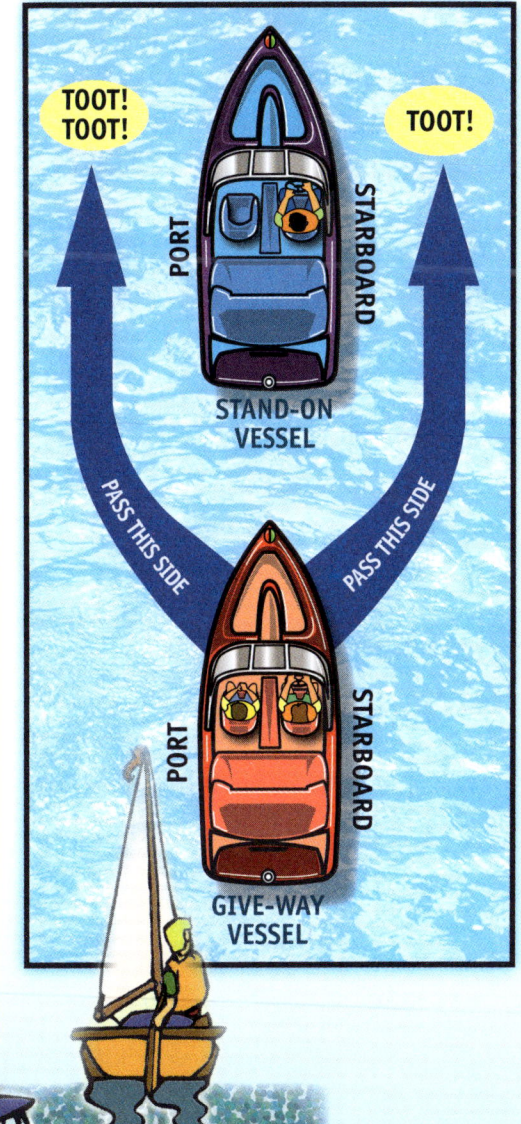

"There's a sailboat, Mr. Catchum. Are we still the Give-way Vessel?"

"Yes Megan. Especially with an unpowered vessel. We'll let them know with a sound signal that we intend to pass."

SidekicksOnCourse.com

5

NAVIGATION RULES

MEETING ANOTHER BOAT

The U.S. Coast Guard's Inland Navigation Rule #14 tells a boater what they need to do in order to properly and safely meet another boat head-on. Meeting another boat means that both boats are on the same straight course where their bows are pointed towards each other.

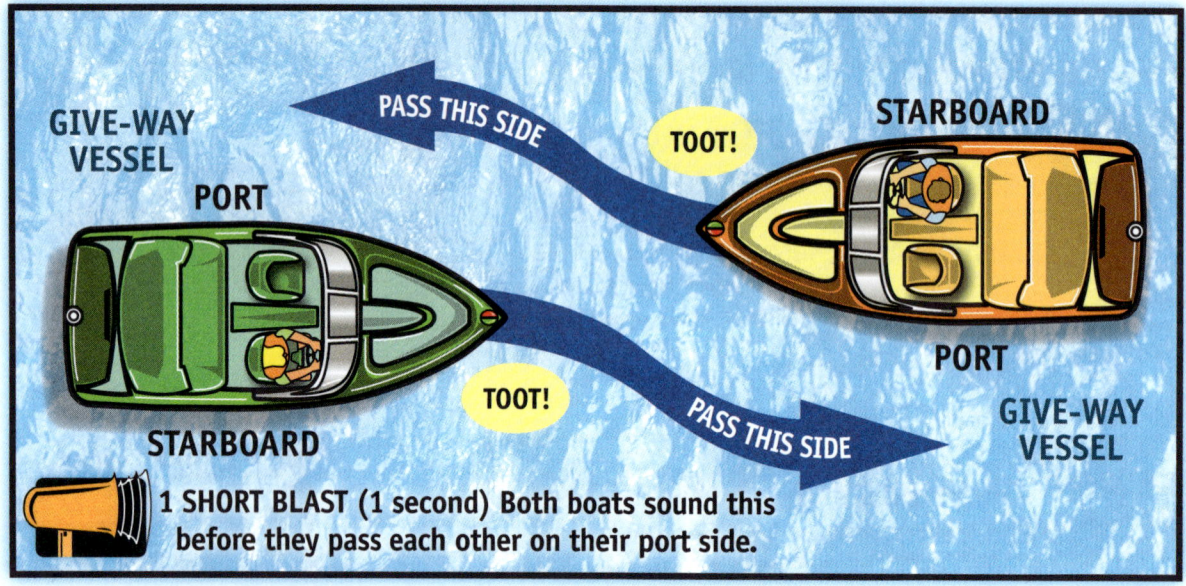

1 SHORT BLAST (1 second) Both boats sound this before they pass each other on their port side.

Have fun unscrambling these three navigation words. *Answer on page 15.*

F A T ◯◯◯   L I O N S C O I L ◯◯◯◯◯◯◯◯◯◯   O B W ◯◯◯

CROSSING ANOTHER BOAT

The U.S. Coast Guard's Navigation Rule #15 tells a boater what they need to do in order to properly and safely cross in front of or behind another boat. Overtaking another boat has both boats going in the same direction. Meeting another boat has both boats approaching each other. Crossing is very different. Crossing another boat depends on whether the other boat is approaching on your left (port) or right (starboard) side.

1 SHORT BLAST (1 second) Both boats sound this as they proceed. *(Inland Rule #34)*

STAND-ON VESSEL — STARBOARD / PORT

TOOT!

GIVE-WAY VESSEL — PORT / STARBOARD

TOOT!

CROSS BEHIND THE OTHER BOAT

Have more fun unscrambling these three navigation words.
Answer on page 15.

LERUS ○○○○○   OTRP ○○○○   ETRSN ○○○○○

"WOW, Mr. Catchum, that boater doesn't see you!"

"You're right, Oscar. That's why there are navigation rules for crossing."

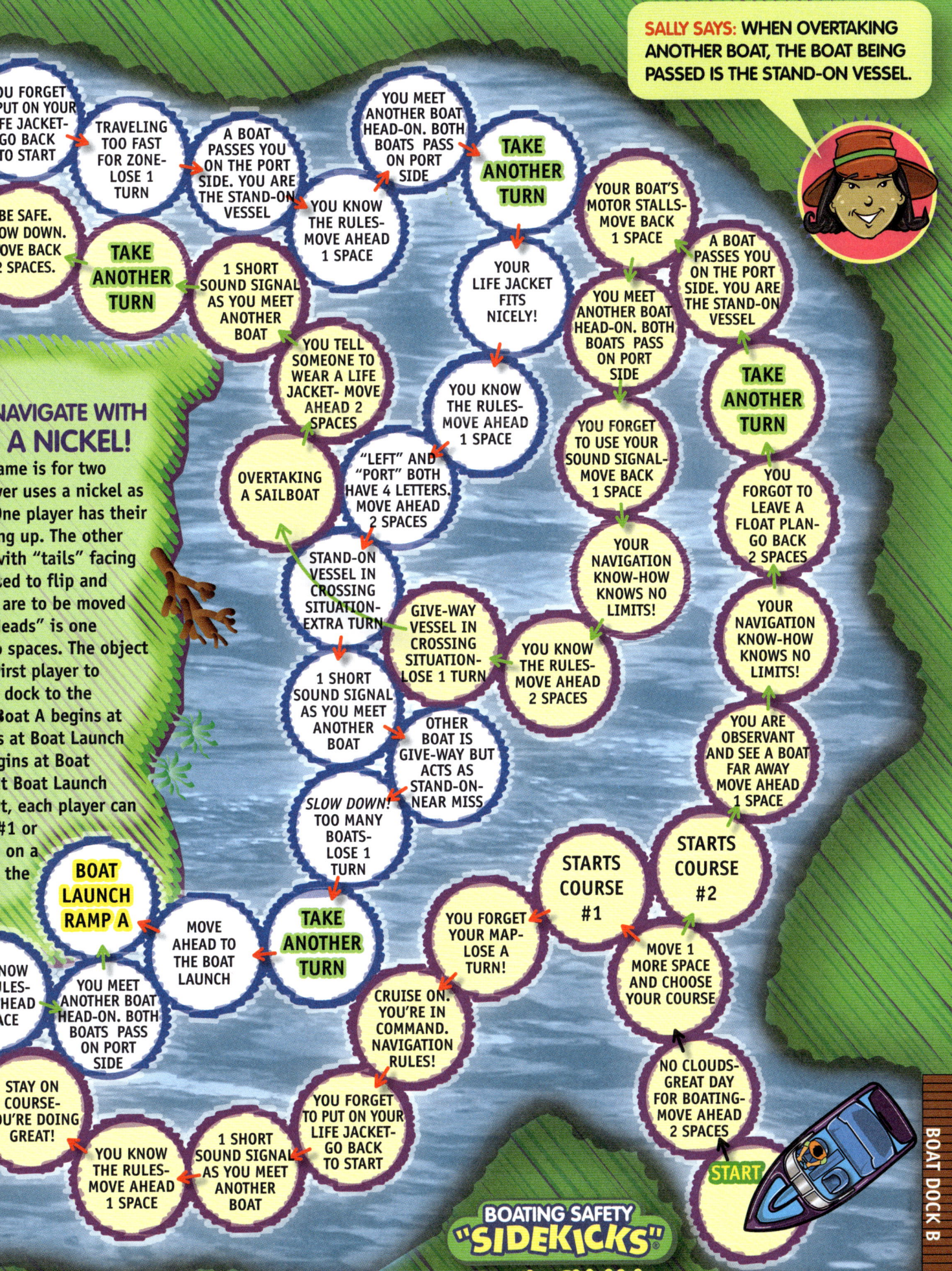

NAVIGATION RULES

ON THE WATER TOGETHER!

Bicycles, motorcycles, cars, trucks and large tractor-trailers are vehicle traffic on streets. Open waters are the same. Everyone from paddlers of kayaks and canoes to sailboats to powerboats to large cabin cruisers to large cargo vessels navigate on boating waters. How do all these different vessels boat around each other? They are all supposed to know the navigation rules. And the navigation rules apply to all boats. While it's that simple, it means that all boaters need to follow these rules to boat safely. The main reason to follow the navigation rules is to avoid a collision.

Match these types of boats with their pictures above.

A. PONTOON B. CANOE C. JONBOAT D. PERSONAL WATERCRAFT E. ROWBOAT
F. KAYAK G. CABIN CRUISER H. JET BOAT I. POWERBOAT J. SAILBOAT

Answers on page 15.

NAVIGATION RULES

SAFE SPEED AND LOOKOUT
GIVE-WAY VESSEL

The U.S. Coast Guard's Inland Navigation Rule #16 says that the boat which is to keep out of the way of another vessel is the Give-way Vessel. This boat is to take action to keep out of the way of other vessels. All vessels must change course, slow down or stop to avoid a collision between boats. Navigation Rule #5 says that all boats must maintain a proper lookout to avoid collisions. This means that boaters need to look and listen around them at all times.

IN FRONT OF YOU

Each of the views below is for the Give-way Vessel. For each view, check the box if the vessel is in an overtaking (passing), meeting or crossing navigation situation.

Answers on page 15.

☐ overtaking ☐ meeting ☐ crossing
You sound 1 short blast.
You hear 1 short blast.

☐ overtaking ☐ meeting ☐ crossing
You sound 1 short blast.
You hear 1 short blast.

☐ overtaking ☐ meeting ☐ crossing
You sound 1 short blast.
You hear 1 short blast.

☐ overtaking ☐ meeting ☐ crossing
You sound 2 short blasts.
You hear 2 short blasts.

SidekicksOnCourse.com

NAVIGATION RULES

SAFE SPEED AND LOOKOUT
STAND-ON VESSEL

The U.S. Coast Guard's Inland Navigation Rule #17 says that the Stand-on Vessel is to maintain or keep its course (direction) and speed. The Stand-on Vessel must do this while the Give-way Vessel keeps out of its way. In the event a Stand-on Vessel is approaching a possible collision, it can take action as a Give-way Vessel to avoid the collision. When crossing with an unpowered boat, the powered boat is the Give-way Vessel.

IN FRONT OF YOU

Each of the views below is for the Stand-on Vessel. For each view, check the box if the vessel is in an overtaking (passing), meeting or crossing navigation situation. *Answers on page 15.*

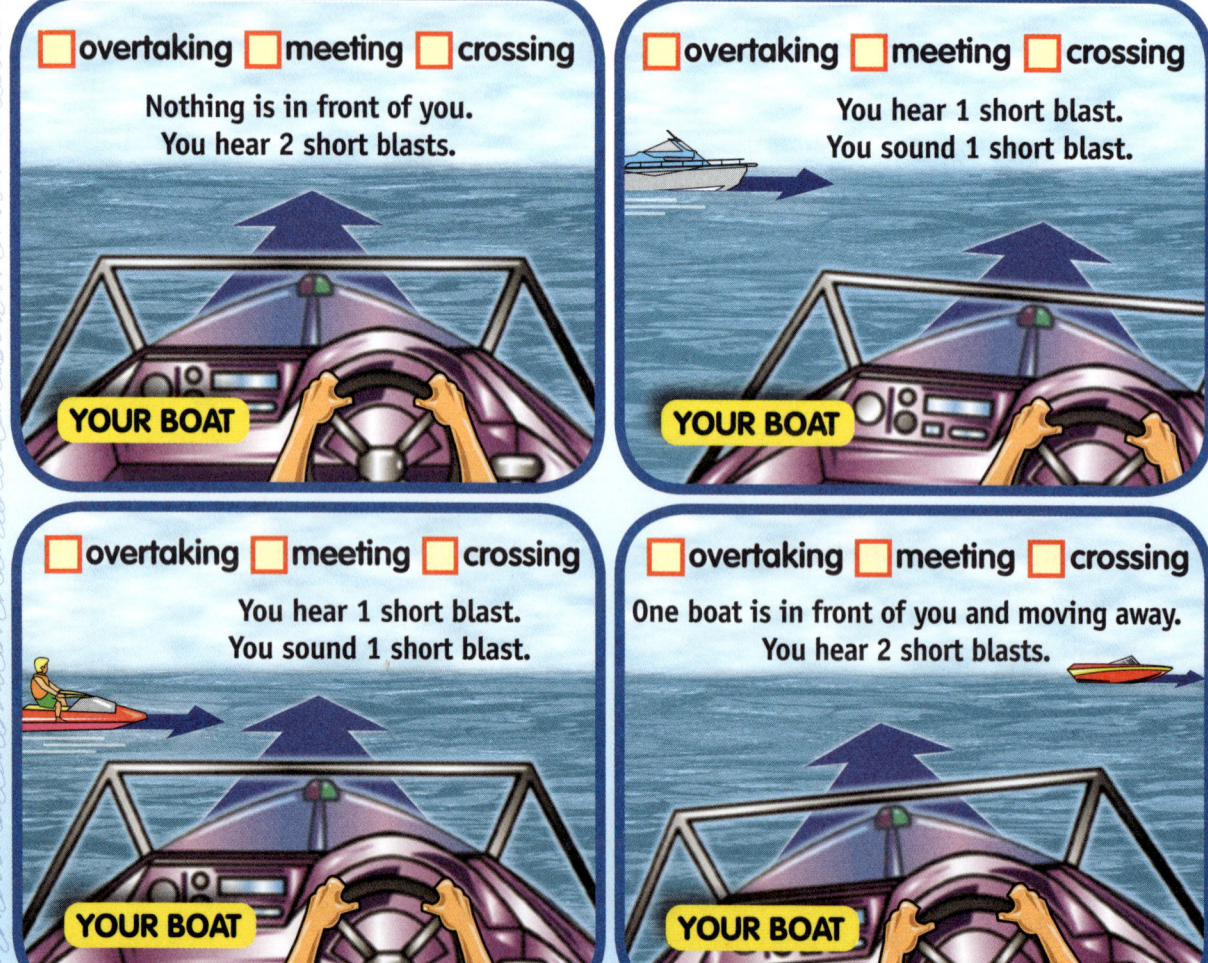

☐ overtaking ☐ meeting ☐ crossing
Nothing is in front of you.
You hear 2 short blasts.

☐ overtaking ☐ meeting ☐ crossing
You hear 1 short blast.
You sound 1 short blast.

☐ overtaking ☐ meeting ☐ crossing
You hear 1 short blast.
You sound 1 short blast.

☐ overtaking ☐ meeting ☐ crossing
One boat is in front of you and moving away.
You hear 2 short blasts.

12 **SidekicksonCourse.com**

NAVIGATION RULES

KEEP YOUR DISTANCE

Navigation rules are followed to prevent collisions. Each boat operator is required to maintain a proper lookout and follow these rules. Boaters are also required to follow other rules. One of these is keeping our waterways safe and secure.

3 FEET = 1 YARD
100 YARDS = 300 FEET
500 YARDS = 1,500 FEET

OPERATE AT MINIMUM SPEED

BOAT OPERATORS MUST:
- Keep their distance from all military, cruise line or commercial shipping vessels! Boaters are not to approach these vessels within 100 yards.
- Within 500 yards of any large U.S. naval vessel, including any U.S. military or military supply vessel over 100 feet, boaters are to proceed at a low to minimum speed.

Violators of the Naval Vessel Protection Zone face up to 6 years in prison and a $250,000 fine, not to mention an immediate security check. Approaching certain other commercial vessels may result in an immediate boarding, so keep well away of shipping or cruise line traffic.

FAST FACT: Did you know that sounding five short rapid blasts is the danger signal? Sounding this danger signal when you are not certain what the other boater intends to do is the way to alert the other vessel of a possible collision.

SECURITY SUDOKU

			20
20		30	40
		40	
30	40	20	

Boaters are to stay at least 100 yards from U.S. naval vessels. To solve the puzzle above, make sure each highlighted group of four blocks totals 100. Also, each row (across and down) needs to also total 100.
Answers appear on page 15.

Answers from crossword puzzle on page 14.

SidekicksOnCourse.com

13

NAVIGATION CROSSWORD

ACROSS

1. When two boats are crossing, the boat to the _____ is the Give-way Vessel.
2. Always wear your life _____.
3. The back of the boat is the _____.
4. Rule 15 applies to _____ another boat.
5. A boat that maintains a constant speed and direction is a _____ Vessel.
6. Always keep a proper _____.
7. Operating a boat safely requires knowing the navigation _____.
8. Life jackets must be U.S. _____-approved.
9. While boating, maintain a safe _____.

OBSERVE IT!

SOUND IT!

10. (DOWN) Continue to learn more to stay on _____.

DOWN

1. A boat that stays out of the way of another boat is a _____ Vessel.
2. The left side of the boat is _____.
3. Rule 14 applies to _____ another boat.
4. Navigation rules help prevent boat _____.
5. Rule 13 applies to _____ another boat.
6. Keep the legal distance from U.S. _____ vessels.
7. Boaters sometimes call navigation rules the "Rules of the _____."
8. The front of the boat is the _____.
9. The right side of the boat is _____.

WEAR IT!

Answers to crossword puzzle on page 13.

NAVIGATION RULES

TYPE 1: Intended for offshore use.
TYPE 2: Near-shore buoyancy vests.
TYPE 3: Flotation Aid.
TYPE 4: Throwable devices. These are not to be used as a life jacket.
TYPE 5: These are special use life jackets.
INFLATABLES: Life Jackets, Belt Packs

"SIDEKICKS" WEAR IT!

LIFE JACKETS SAVE LIVES.

On average, 90% of those who drown while boating were not wearing a life jacket. The first rule of safe boating is to wear a life jacket at all times when on or near the water. Read the life jacket's label, and make sure it's U.S. Coast Guard approved. The right fit provides the right flotation. *Remember, it doesn't work if you don't wear it!*

Be safe and keep your life jacket snug.
Buckle up! Zip up!

NAVIGATION WORDS YOU NEED TO KNOW

AFT- on a boat, the direction near or at the back of the boat (stern).
AIDS TO NAVIGATION (ATON)- Markers and buoys in the water that assist boaters in determining their position or safe course, or to warn them of dangers or obstructions that can be found on a chart.
BOW- It's the front of a boat.
BUOYS- These are like road signs on the water, they can show the edges of water channels, directions, hazards and areas where boats are to stay away.
CHANNEL- It's a portion of a waterway marked with buoys or markers.
FORWARD- On a boat, it's the direction towards the front (bow).
GIVE-WAY VESSEL- It's a boat which stays out of the way of the Stand-on Vessel when meeting, overtaking or crossing.

HEADING- It's the direction a boat is pointed.
HULL- The structure or structural body of a boat.
LIFE JACKET- Personal Flotation Device (PFD). The most important item you can have on a boat. A lifesaving must–wear it!
PORT- The left side of a boat.
SOUND SIGNALS- Using a whistle, horn or bell, it is a way to safely let other boaters know how you change course.
STAND-ON VESSEL- A boat that maintains a constant speed and direction over the Give-way Vessel when meeting, overtaking or passing.
STARBOARD- The right side of a boat.
STERN- It's the back of a boat.
TRANSOM- It's the flat part of the stern.
WAKE- A wave or rippling of water caused by a boat's passage as it travels through the water.

ANSWER KEY
Page 4: BOATS A/E, B/G, C/D, F doesn't have a match.
Page 5: GIVEWAY PASSES STANDON
Page 6: AFT, COLLISION, BOW
Page 7: RULES, PORT, STERN
Page 10: 1. CABIN CRUISER 2. CANOE 3. JET BOAT 4. KAYAK 5. ROWBOAT 6. SAILBOAT 7. POWERBOAT 8. PONTOON 9. JONBOAT 10. PERSONAL WATERCRAFT
Page 11: meeting; overtaking; crossing; overtaking
Page 12: overtaking; crossing; crossing; overtaking, the boat in front of you is moving away, but there's a boat approaching from behind your boat.

Page 13

40	30	10	20
20	10	30	40
10	20	40	30
30	40	20	10

ISBN 978-0-9718864-6-9   text and illustrations: Within Reach Inc.

SidekicksonCourse.com

SidekicksonCourse.com

STAY ON COURSE with knowledge and fun that takes you to the watery world of safe boating. Knowledge is the key to safer boating. Let the Boating Safety Sidekicks show you the way.

Kids identify with kids. That's why the National Safe Boating Council's Boating Safety Sidekicks has succeeded for more than 10 years in bringing kids into the adopted realm of safe boating with this cartoon team. Youth are the spark of the next generation of safe boating and ardent life jacket wear. This publication is provided for kids to enjoy on their own or with the help of an adult. We hope that you'll share this with many other future boaters.

National Safe Boating Council
P.O. Box 509
Bristow, VA 20136

www.SafeBoatingCouncil.org
www.BoatingSidekicks.com

YOUR BOATING DOLLARS AT WORK

Produced under a grant from the Sport Fish Restoration and Boating Trust Fund, administered by the U.S. Coast Guard.

Sponsored by the
Virginia Department of Game & Inland Fisheries

For more information on safe boating, visit our web site at:

www.dgif.virginia.gov

ISBN: 978-0-9718864-6-9

printed on recycled paper with soy-based inks

Use your smartphone, a QR code app and scan this QR code to go to www.SidekicksOnCourse.com.